Pearl Harbor

Tamara L. Britton
ABDO Publishing Company

visit us at
www.abdopub.com

Published by ABDO Publishing Company, 4940 Viking Drive, Edina, Minnesota 55435.
Copyright © 2003 by Abdo Consulting Group, Inc. International copyrights reserved in
all countries. No part of this book may be reproduced in any form without written
permission from the publisher.

Printed in the United States of America

Editors: Kate A. Conley, Kristy Langanki Cannon, Kristianne E. Vieregger
Photo Credits: AP/Wide World, Corbis
Art Direction & Maps: Neil Klinepier

Library of Congress Cataloging-in-Publication Data

Britton, Tamara L., 1963-
    Pearl Harbor / Tamara L. Britton.
        p. cm. -- (Symbols, landmarks, and monuments)
    Includes index.
    Summary: Presents an overview of the history of Pearl Harbor, Hawaii, including the
1941 Japanese attack during World War II and the establishment of the U.S.S. Arizona
Memorial.
    ISBN 1-57765-851-5
        1. Pearl Harbor (Hawaii), Attack on, 1941--Juvenile literature. 2. USS Arizona
Memorial (Hawaii)--Juvenile literature. 3. World War, 1939-1945--United States--
Hawaii--Juvenile literature. [1. Pearl Harbor (Hawaii) 2. Pearl Harbor (Hawaii), Attack
on, 1941. 3. USS Arizona Memorial (Hawaii) 4. World War, 1939-1945--United States.]
    I. Title.

D767.92 .B68 2002
940.54'26--dc21

                                                                2002066663

Contents

Pearl Harbor

On December 7, 1941, Japanese troops attacked Pearl Harbor, Hawaii, and its naval station. Many people died, and many navy ships were lost. The attack brought the United States into World War II.

Pearl Harbor was not always a naval station, however. For hundreds of years, native Hawaiians fished and caught oysters in this harbor. Later, European explorers discovered the harbor. Soon, Pearl Harbor was a center of business for the trade routes in the Pacific Ocean.

The USS Arizona *Memorial in Pearl Harbor*

In the late nineteenth century, the United States built military bases at Pearl Harbor. U.S. leaders recognized the harbor's location as a good place for a naval station. They made Pearl Harbor home of the U.S. Navy's Pacific **Fleet**.

Over the years, the U.S. Navy has greatly developed Pearl Harbor.

After the Allies' victory in World War II, Pearl Harbor's naval station was repaired. But many people believed there should be a **memorial** to all who died in the Japanese attack and the war.

So Hawaii started a program to create memorials. Many people wanted to build a memorial at the USS *Arizona*. More than 1,700 sailors died when this ship sunk. In 1962, the USS *Arizona* Memorial was **dedicated**.

The memorials in Pearl Harbor honor those who lost their lives in the Japanese attack and in World War II. Through these sites, people from all over the world remember the sacrifices made by those who died in selfless service to their countries. Because of this, Pearl Harbor and its memorials are some of the nation's most important **landmarks** and monuments.

The USS Arizona *Memorial is one of many memorials at Pearl Harbor.*

Fast Facts

√ As many as 1.5 million people visit Pearl Harbor every year.

√ The Japanese attack on Pearl Harbor lasted for almost two hours.

√ Several movies have shown the events of December 7, 1941.

√ The USS *Arizona* Memorial is one of 120 military memorials in the National Park system, and one of the most frequently visited in the country.

√ The U.S. flag is still raised over the USS *Arizona* Memorial every day.

√ Many artifacts from December 7, 1941, were recovered from Pearl Harbor after the attack and are on display in the museum.

√ After the war, Elvis Presley played a benefit concert in Hawaii to help raise money for the USS *Arizona* Memorial.

Timeline

1941   √   On December 7, just before 8 A.M., Japan attacks Pearl Harbor.
       √   On December 8, the United States declares war on Japan.

1945   √   World War II ends on September 2.

1949   √   The Pacific War Memorial Commission is formed to raise money for Pearl Harbor memorials.

1950   √   The navy begins raising the U.S. flag over the USS *Arizona* every day.

1955   √   The first permanent memorial is dedicated on December 7.

1962   √   The USS *Arizona* Memorial is dedicated on Memorial Day.

1972   √   A memorial is dedicated at the USS *Utah*.

1998   √   The USS *Missouri* comes to Pearl Harbor.

A Shelter in the Sea

Hawaii is a group of islands in the South Pacific. Pearl Harbor is a natural harbor on Hawaii's Oahu Island. Hawaiians called the harbor Wai Momi. This means Pearl Waters in the native Hawaiian language. Many pearl oysters lived in the harbor.

Native Hawaiians harvested the oysters and caught fish in the harbor. They believed the shark goddess Ka'ahupahau and her brother Kahi'uka lived in the harbor's waters. They protected the Hawaiians from the sharks that prowled there.

James Cook

In 1776, Captain James Cook left England to explore America's Pacific coast. He was looking for the **Northwest Passage**. Two years later, on his way

10

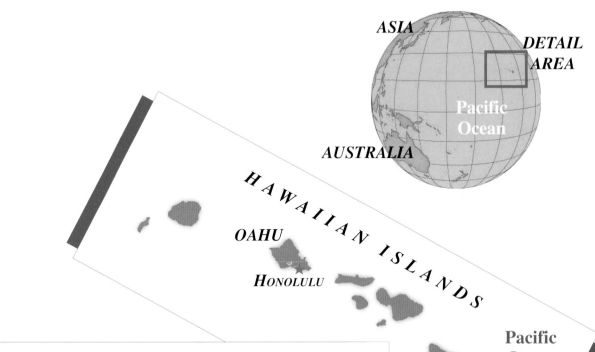

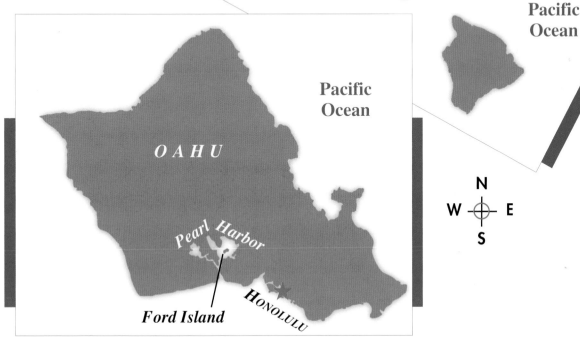

north, Captain Cook discovered Hawaii. He called the islands the Sandwich Islands.

After Captain Cook came to Hawaii, it became a center of trade in the South Pacific. Soon **missionaries** and businessmen arrived from the United States. Pearl Harbor became a busy port.

In 1887, the United States and Hawaii signed a treaty. The treaty said the United States could build a coal station at Pearl Harbor. The coal station would refuel and repair ships traveling on the Pacific trade routes. In exchange, Hawaii could export sugar to the United States without paying taxes.

The influence of U.S. business and missionary work weakened Hawaii's government. In 1898, the United States **annexed** the Hawaiian Islands. In 1900, Hawaii became a U.S. territory.

James Cook died in Hawaii after a battle between his men and the native Hawaiians.

Naval Station

The United States thought that Pearl Harbor would be an excellent place for a naval station. In 1899, the U.S. Navy took control of the coal station. In November of that year, a naval station was officially established.

In 1901, the U.S. government passed the Appropriation Act. This act gave the navy money to buy the land surrounding the harbor. Then the navy built ship-repair facilities, housing, and a water system. The harbor was **dredged** so that big ships could sail in through the entrance.

During this time, the U.S. Army also had bases in the Pearl Harbor area. Some army leaders thought the army should have control of Pearl Harbor. And other government departments were claiming parts of the harbor's land as well. For example, the Department of Agriculture and the Department of Labor and Commerce claimed land for projects of their own.

Navy leaders did not believe this was fair. They realized Pearl Harbor's value as a naval station. And the navy was spending money to improve the harbor. In 1908, the Pearl Harbor naval station was completed. Soon, businesses and private citizens could not use the harbor anymore.

In 1919, the navy bought Ford Island. Ford Island is a 450-acre (182-ha) island in the middle of the harbor. It was named after Dr. Seth Ford, a Honolulu physician. The navy built Luke Field on the island. The navy shared the base with the army. In 1920, the Naval Air Station was built there.

By 1934, the navy had spent more than $42 million on the Pearl Harbor naval station. In 1935, military operations were organized into two units, the island district and the naval station. The island district was responsible for base operations, security, and the people who kept the ships in good order. The naval station was responsible for operation of the naval ships.

By 1941, Pearl Harbor was named home to the U.S. Navy's Pacific **Fleet**. There was also a naval air base, a submarine base, a marine base, army bases, and a PT boat base at Pearl Harbor.

Ford Island still looks much like it did during World War II.

17

The World at War

World War II began when Germany invaded Poland in 1939. Then Britain and France declared war on Germany in support of Poland. Soon, many other countries became involved in the war.

In 1940, Germany, Italy, and Japan signed the Tripartite Pact. It established these three countries and their **allies** as the Axis powers. They supported each other's efforts to conquer neighboring countries.

Other countries, led by Britain and France, were called the Allies. They joined together to fight the Axis powers. But the Allies needed help against such powerful opponents. So they asked the United States for aid.

This famous photograph shows the USS Shaw *exploding on December 7, 1941.*

Many Americans did not want the United States to enter the war. So the U.S. government passed the Lend-Lease Act in 1941. Under this act, the United States could send aid to nations under Axis attack.

The USS Arizona *as it burns in Pearl Harbor*

In July of 1941, the U.S. government froze Japanese **assets** in the United States. They did this in response to Japan's actions to overtake its neighboring countries. The United States also stopped shipments of **petroleum** products to Japan.

Tojo Hideki

The U.S. actions upset Japan's leaders. So Prime Minister Tojo Hideki decided to attack the United States. Many Japanese people did not want to go to war with the United States. They wanted to find a peaceful solution to the conflicts between the countries.

But Japan's leaders wanted to destroy the U.S. Naval **Fleet** in the Pacific. They thought this would allow Japan to easily expand into the South Pacific. And they wanted to pay back the United States for freezing Japan's assets in the United States.

Admiral Yamamoto Isoroku was commander in chief of Japan's fleet. Japan's government asked him to plan the attack on the United States. Yamamoto did not believe the attack was a good idea. He knew the United States was a powerful nation. He believed Japan would lose if the war lasted more than a year.

But Yamamoto had to follow the orders of Japan's leaders. So he thought about the attack. He decided the best chance of a Japanese victory was to attack the United States by surprise. So he planned a secret attack on the Pearl Harbor naval station.

On November 26, 1941, a **fleet** of Japanese navy ships sailed to an area north of Hawaii. There, about 360 planes on six aircraft carriers waited for the attack to begin.

Yamamoto Isoroku

21

December 7, 1941

On December 7, 1941, shortly before 8:00 A.M., Japanese planes flew into Pearl Harbor. The pilots found that almost the entire U.S. Pacific **Fleet** was anchored in the harbor. The ships were waiting to be inspected.

Japanese bombers before the attack

There were 130 U.S. Navy ships in Pearl Harbor. Eight of them were battleships. There were also nine cruisers, 29 destroyers, and five submarines.

The USS Virginia, Tennessee, *and* Arizona *burning on December 7, 1941*

The Japanese dropped bombs on the ships. They dropped torpedoes into the water near the ships. The Japanese pilots also dropped bombs on nearby U.S. Army, Air Force, and Marine bases.

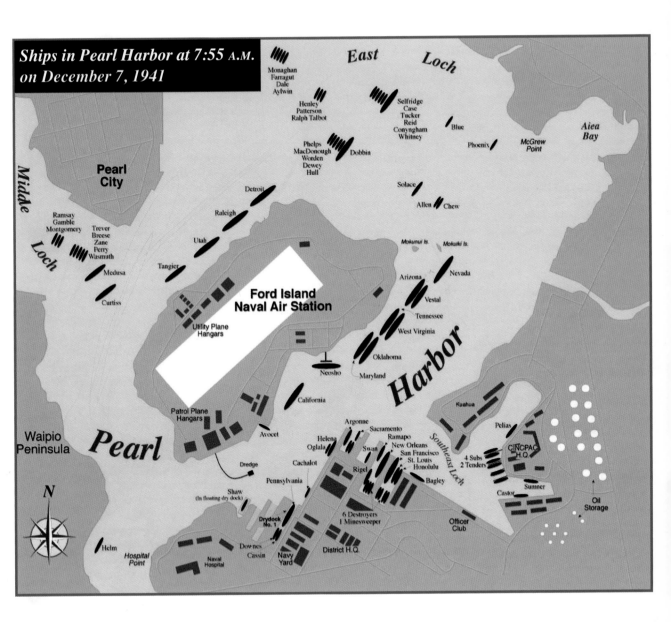

Ships in Pearl Harbor at 7:55 A.M. on December 7, 1941

East Loch

Monaghan
Farragut
Dale
Aylwin

Henley
Patterson
Ralph Talbot

Selfridge
Case
Tucker
Reid
Conyngham
Whitney

Blue

Aiea Bay

Phelps
MacDonough
Worden
Dewey
Hull

Dobbin

Phoenix

McGrew Point

Pearl City

Detroit

Solace

Ramsay
Gamble
Montgomery

Trever
Breese
Zane
Perry
Wasmuth

Raleigh

Allen Chew

Utah

Mokunui Is.   Mokuiki Is.

Middle Loch

Medusa

Tangier

Arizona   Nevada

Curtiss

Vestal

Ford Island Naval Air Station

Tennessee

West Virginia

Utility Plane Hangars

Neosho

Oklahoma

Maryland

Harbor

California

Kuahua

Patrol Plane Hangars

Argonne

Pelias

Avocet

Sacramento
Ramapo
New Orleans
San Francisco
St. Louis
Honolulu

Helena
Oglala

Swan

CINCPAC H.Q.

Waipio Peninsula

Pearl

Dredge

Cachalot

Rigel

Southeast Loch

4 Subs
2 Tenders

Bagley

Pennsylvania

Castor   Sumner

Shaw
(In floating dry dock)

Drydock No. 1

6 Destroyers
1 Minesweeper

Officer Club

Oil Storage

Helm

Hospital Point

Downes
Cassin

Navy Yard

District H.Q.

Naval Hospital

N

23

The attack ended at about 10 A.M. Twenty-one ships were damaged or sunk. One hundred eighty-eight planes were destroyed, and 159 planes were damaged. The attack killed 2,403 U.S. military personnel and wounded 1,178 others. Forty-nine civilians died, and 83 others were wounded. The Japanese lost 29 planes, 55 pilots, and five submarines.

On December 8, 1941, the U.S. **Congress** declared war on Japan. Now, the United States entered World War II. The U.S. Pacific **Fleet** was quickly rebuilt. American forces joined the Allies in the war against the Axis powers.

The war was a long, hard struggle. Thousands of troops on both sides were killed. American soldiers rallied around the cry "Remember Pearl Harbor!" They wanted to avenge the people who died in the attack.

Eventually, the Allies took control. On June 6, 1944, troops landed on the beaches of Normandy, France. This is called D-Day. They began liberating countries from German control. On May 7, 1945, Germany surrendered. May 8 is called VE (Victory in Europe) Day. Soon the Allies had freed Europe from Axis control.

But the Japanese continued to fight. So U.S. leaders dropped **nuclear** bombs on Nagasaki and Hiroshima, Japan. Japan surrendered to the Allies on August 14, 1945. August 15 is called VJ (Victory over Japan) Day. On September 2, 1945, World War II officially ended when Japanese leaders signed a surrender treaty on the USS *Missouri*.

President Franklin D. Roosevelt signs the war declaration.

Memorials

After the war, many people thought there should be **memorials** at Pearl Harbor. They wanted to honor those who lost their lives on December 7, 1941. So in 1949, Hawaii established the Pacific War Memorial Commission (PWMC). It would raise money to build the memorials.

In 1951, the PWMC decided to build a series of memorials. Sites that would receive memorials included Red Hill, the U.S. Marine parade ground, the main gate of Pearl Harbor Naval Air Station, and the USS *Arizona*.

On December 7, 1955, a plaque on Ford Island was **dedicated**. This plaque was Pearl Harbor's first permanent memorial.

Of the vessels damaged in the Pearl Harbor attack, only the USS *Arizona* was permanently lost. A bomb had landed

The U.S. flag is raised on the USS Arizona *Memorial (left). A World War II veteran stands in the Shrine Room (above).*

in its **ammunition** storage area. The ship sank in less than nine minutes. This ship lost more than 1,700 men.

Many people wanted a special **memorial** to honor this massive loss of life on the USS *Arizona*. In 1950, the U.S. Navy began to raise and lower the American flag over the wreck every day. They did this as a sign of respect for the lost crewmen.

Before 1958, the U.S. Navy could only accept money from the U.S. Treasury. That year, the government passed a law that allowed the navy to accept money from other sources. So the PWMC began to raise funds for the USS *Arizona* Memorial. It raised more than $500,000.

The USS Arizona Memorial

The PWMC hired **architect** Alfred Preis to design the USS *Arizona* **Memorial**. He designed a 184-foot (56-m) long white building. The building spans the sunken ship but does not touch it. The USS *Arizona* Memorial was **dedicated** on Memorial Day in 1962.

Visitors to the **memorial** first stop at the visitor center to get a ticket. A U.S. Navy launch boat takes visitors to the memorial. While waiting for the boat, visitors can see **artifacts** from the ship in the memorial's museum.

At the memorial, visitors first go through the Entry. In the Entry's flag room, flags of all the battleships that were in the harbor on December 7, 1941, are on display. At the other end of the room are the U.S. and State of Hawaii flags. The flags of the armed services are on display, too.

People stand in line at the USS Arizona Memorial Entry (opposite page and right).

From the Entry, visitors go into the Assembly Room. The Assembly is a long room with windows on both sides. Here, the USS *Arizona* can best be seen. Diagrams help visitors identify parts of the ship that they can see above the water.

From the Assembly, visitors enter the Shrine Room. There, the names of all the USS *Arizona*'s crew that died on December 7, 1941, are carved on the marble walls. A smaller **memorial** near the U.S. flag has the names of survivors of the attack that have since died.

A visitor center at the USS *Arizona* Memorial opened in 1980. That same year, the National Park Service took control of the memorial. More than 1.5 million people visit the memorial and visitor center each year.

The USS *Arizona* was not the last memorial built at Pearl Harbor. In 1972, a memorial was **dedicated** at the USS *Utah*. The USS *Utah* was sunk on the other side of Ford Island. The USS *Utah* is the only other ship still underwater at Pearl Harbor. There are 58 crewmen buried there.

In 1998, the USS *Missouri* came to Pearl Harbor. It opened to the public on January 29, 1999. The USS *Missouri* is a **memorial** and a museum. There, visitors can see the place where Japan signed the treaty that ended World War II.

Visiting the Shrine Room can be an emotional experience for many people.

The Assembly Room

Pearl Harbor Today

Today, Pearl Harbor has a naval shipyard and a submarine base. Many soldiers are still stationed there. The military and the National Park Service work to maintain the harbor and its **memorials**.

As time passes, this becomes more challenging. The USS *Arizona* had 1 million gallons (3.8 million liters) of oil in its fuel tanks when it sunk. Drops of oil from the wreck rise to the surface of the water every few seconds.

Park Service officials fear that the ship is **deteriorating**. This could cause the ship to collapse. Then all the oil would be released into the harbor. So in 1983, the Park Service hired divers to study the ship's condition.

The divers mapped the USS *Arizona's* resting site. They found that the ship had more damage than expected. They also found some bombs that had not exploded during the attack. And they found a sunken Japanese submarine.

The Shrine Room

By the mid-1990s, the USS *Arizona*'s oil was leaking more rapidly. The Park Service began monitoring the ship using remote-operated **vehicles**. This allowed officials to see inside the ship. Then they could more closely monitor the USS *Arizona*'s condition.

But **deterioration** is not the only threat to Pearl Harbor's **memorials**. The U.S. Navy plans to build housing, businesses, and recreational facilities on Ford Island. The Admiral Clarey Bridge opened in 1988. Now, for the first time, Ford Island is linked with the Oahu Island by road.

Park officials fear the bridge and new developments will increase the number of people traveling to Ford Island. This could increase the chances of theft of **artifacts**. So park officials are busy mapping historical sites, including the USS *Arizona*. And they are considering **installing** a security camera system.

The day after the attack on Pearl Harbor, President Franklin D. Roosevelt gave a speech to **Congress**. He said December 7, 1941, was ". . . a date which will live in infamy . . ." President Roosevelt knew that Americans would always "Remember Pearl Harbor!"

Pearl Harbor and its **memorials** are symbols of not only that tragic day, but also of courage and sacrifice. These memorials honor the thousands of men and women who served their country during World War II.

Ford Island today

Glossary

allies - countries that agree to help each other in times of need.

ammunition - bullets, shells, and other items used in firearms.

annex - to add land to a nation.

architect - a person who plans and designs buildings.

artifact - anything made by humans a long time ago.

asset - something of value. When a government freezes assets, it is stopping the use or production of the assets.

Congress - the lawmaking body of the United States. It is made up of the Senate and the House of Representatives. It meets in Washington, D.C.

dedicate - to open to public use.

deteriorate - to become or make worse.

dredge - to deepen.

fleet - a group of warships under one command.

install - to put in place for use.

landmark - an important structure of historical or physical interest.

memorial - something that stands as a reminder of a person or event.

missionary - a person who spreads a church's religion.

Northwest Passage - a passage by sea between the Pacific and the Atlantic Oceans along the north coast of North America.

nuclear - of or relating to atomic energy.

petroleum - a thick, yellowish-black oil. It is the source of gasoline.

vehicle - any device used for carrying persons or objects.

Web Sites

Would you like to learn more about Pearl Harbor and World War II?
Please visit **www.abdopub.com** to find up-to-date Web site links with
great information about Pearl Harbor, including stories from people who
were really there. These links are routinely monitored and updated to
provide the most current information available.

Fireworks go off in Pearl Harbor on VJ Day, August 15, 1945.

Index